7 REMOTE SIDE HUSTLES YOU CAN START IN 2025

JAMES D JOHN

© 2024 JAMES D JOHN

All rights reserved.

No part of this book may be reproduced, stored in a retrieval system, or transmitted in any form or by any means, electronic, mechanical, photocopying, recording, or otherwise, without the prior written permission of the author, except for brief quotations used in critical reviews or articles.

Disclaimer

This book is intended for informational purposes only. The information contained herein is based on the author's research, analysis, and interpretation of available data at the time of publication. While every effort has been made to ensure the accuracy of the content, the author, publisher, and any associated entities make no guarantees about the accuracy, completeness, or suitability of the information for any particular purpose.

Table of Contents

INTRODUCTION 1
Chapter 1: 9
Key Drivers of Inflation Increase 9
    Impact of Motor Fuels and Clothing Prices 10
    Role of Core Inflation and Services Inflation 12
Chapter 2: 19
Bank of England's Monetary Policy Response 19
    Monetary Policy Committee Meeting Outlook 19
    Interest Rate Trends and Market Expectations 21
Chapter 3: 25
Economic Context and Challenges 25
    Shrinking GDP and Business Confidence 25
        Shrinking GDP: A Cause for Concern 25
        Business Confidence Under Strain 27
        Impact on the Services Sector 28

Impact of Rachel Reeves' Budget on Hiring and Inflation 28
- Key Provisions of the Budget 29
- Effects on Hiring 30
- Inflationary Pressures 31
- Policy Debate and Criticism 32
- Long-Term Implications 33

Chapter 4: 34

Stakeholder Perspectives 34
- Commentary from Economic Experts 35
- Statements from Government Officials 39

Chapter 5: 44

Long-Term Inflationary Concerns 44
- Persistence of Services Inflation 44
- National Insurance Contributions and Services Sector Costs 47
- Broader Implications for Inflation and Economic Policy 51
- Conclusion 53

Chapter 6: ...... **Error! Bookmark not defined.**

Essay Writing Tutoring – Helping Students Succeed**Error! Bookmark not defined.**

Who Needs Essay Tutors? Identifying Your Market**Error! Bookmark not defined.**

Tools to Share and Review Work (Google Docs, Zoom) ....**Error! Bookmark not defined.**

Chapter 6: 54

Forecasts and Projections 54

    Inflation Trajectory for Early 2024 54

    Potential Policy Adjustments by the Bank of England . 57

    Risks and Uncertainties 61

    Conclusion 62

Conclusion 63

INTRODUCTION

Inflation is a vital economic indicator that gauges the rate at which the general level of prices for goods and services rises, thereby eroding purchasing power. In the United Kingdom, inflation trends not only influence household budgets but also guide monetary policy and economic planning. November's inflation data offered fresh insights into the state of the UK economy, signaling both progress and persistent challenges.

The inflation landscape in November 2024 was marked by a rise in the Consumer Price Index (CPI) to 2.6%, up from 2.3% in October. This increase, though modest, underscores the ongoing complexities faced by the Bank of England (BoE) as it seeks to balance economic growth with price stability. While inflation has significantly declined from its peak of 11.1% in October 2022, its resurgence raises critical questions about the sustainability of current policies and the broader economic outlook.

Understanding the drivers behind November's inflation, the implications for monetary policy, and the broader economic context is crucial for policymakers, businesses, and households. This analysis explores the factors influencing inflation, the challenges faced by the UK economy, and the broader implications for future policy decisions.

Overview of UK Inflation Trends in November

The UK's inflation dynamics in November were shaped by several factors, including core inflation, services price pressures, and external economic forces. The rise in the Consumer Price Index (CPI) to 2.6% was anticipated by economists and reflects a confluence of both domestic and global drivers.

Headline CPI Increase

November's CPI figure of 2.6% marked a slight but significant uptick from October's 2.3%. Higher prices for motor fuels and clothing were key contributors to this increase. According to the Office for National Statistics (ONS), motor fuel prices rose in response to fluctuating global oil prices, which had a cascading effect on transportation costs and consumer goods. Similarly, the clothing sector experienced price hikes, partly due to seasonal demand and cost pressures in supply chains.

This rise in CPI aligns with forecasts, but its timing—amid broader economic stagnation—complicates the Bank of England's policy trajectory. The November CPI figure extinguished any lingering hopes of an imminent interest rate cut, as inflation remained well above the BoE's target of 2%.

Core Inflation and Services Inflation

Core inflation, which excludes volatile components like energy, food, alcohol, and tobacco, rose to 3.5% in November, up from 3.3% in October. This measure is particularly significant for policymakers as it captures underlying price pressures. Services inflation, a subset closely monitored by the BoE, remained at 5%, unchanged from October but slightly above the central bank's forecast of 4.9%.

Services inflation is a critical gauge of domestic economic conditions, as it reflects wage growth and labor market dynamics. Persistent services price pressures highlight the challenges in achieving the BoE's 2% inflation target. Clare Lombardelli, the BoE's deputy governor, expressed concern over the stubbornly high services inflation, emphasizing its divergence from target-consistent rates.

Historical Perspective and Recent Trends

The November inflation figures must be viewed against the backdrop of recent trends. Inflation in the UK peaked at 11.1% in October 2022, driven by energy price shocks and supply chain disruptions exacerbated by the Russia-Ukraine conflict. Since then, inflation has gradually declined, aided by falling energy prices and a normalization of supply chains. However, the recent uptick in CPI highlights the complexity of navigating the post-pandemic economic landscape.

The contrast between headline and core inflation also underscores the uneven nature of price pressures. While energy prices have stabilized, other components, such as services and wage-driven costs, continue to exert upward pressure. This divergence poses a significant challenge for monetary policymakers tasked with maintaining price stability without stifling economic growth.

Context of Economic Challenges

The UK's inflation dynamics cannot be fully understood without considering the broader economic challenges that frame them. In November 2024, the UK economy faced a confluence of headwinds, including stagnant growth, declining business confidence, and fiscal policy adjustments. These factors not only influenced inflation trends but also shaped the policy responses available to the Bank of England and the government.

Stagnant Economic Growth

The UK's GDP contracted for two consecutive months leading up to November, signaling a stagnating economy. This contraction reflects weak consumer spending, subdued investment, and declining industrial output. Business surveys further highlighted deteriorating confidence and curtailed hiring intentions, exacerbating concerns about the economy's resilience.

The slowdown in economic activity has significant implications for inflation dynamics. A stagnant economy typically exerts downward pressure on prices due to weaker demand. However, the UK's experience in November defied this expectation, as inflationary pressures persisted despite broader economic malaise. This anomaly underscores the complex interplay between supply-side and demand-side factors in shaping inflation.

Fiscal Policy and Labor Market Dynamics

Fiscal policy developments in October 2024, particularly Rachel Reeves' tax-raising Budget, had a pronounced impact on the economy. The Budget included an increase in national insurance contributions for employers, which disproportionately affected the services sector due to its reliance on labor-intensive operations. This policy change added to inflationary pressures by raising labor costs, thereby feeding into services inflation.

The rise in employer national insurance contributions also dampened hiring intentions among businesses, further weakening the labor market.

Historically, tight labor markets have been associated with upward wage pressures, but the UK's current scenario presents a paradox: inflationary wage growth coexists with declining employment prospects. This divergence reflects the uneven impact of fiscal policy changes across sectors and income groups.

External Economic Factors

Global economic conditions also played a role in shaping the UK's inflation trends in November. Fluctuations in global oil prices influenced domestic fuel costs, while lingering supply chain disruptions continued to affect the prices of imported goods. Additionally, the depreciation of the pound sterling, which edged down 0.1% to $1.269 following the release of inflation data, exacerbated import costs and added to inflationary pressures.

The UK's trade and investment flows are further constrained by post-Brexit realities, which have amplified the economy's vulnerability to external shocks. These challenges complicate efforts to stabilize inflation, as external factors often lie beyond the control of domestic policymakers.

Monetary Policy Dilemmas

The Bank of England's monetary policy response to November's inflation data illustrates the dilemmas it faces. With interest rates held steady at 4.75% during the Monetary Policy Committee meeting in December, the BoE signaled caution in light of persistent inflationary pressures. The decision to refrain from cutting rates reflects the central bank's commitment to anchoring inflation expectations, even as economic growth falters.

However, this approach is not without risks. Maintaining high interest rates can suppress borrowing and investment, potentially deepening the economic slowdown. At the same time, the BoE's gradualist approach to policy easing—as articulated by Governor Andrew Bailey—reflects a recognition of the structural challenges underpinning inflation, particularly in the services sector.

Social and Political Implications

The resurgence of inflation in November also has significant social and political implications. Rising prices for essential goods and services strain household budgets, particularly for low-income families already grappling with the cost-of-living crisis. This dynamic adds to the political pressures faced by the government, as calls for targeted interventions to alleviate financial hardship grow louder.

Shadow Chancellor Mel Stride criticized Rachel Reeves' fiscal policies, accusing her of making "irresponsible and inflationary decisions." In response, Reeves highlighted the need to support working families, framing her policies as a means to address longstanding economic inequities. This debate underscores the political stakes associated with inflation management, as policymakers navigate competing priorities of fiscal prudence and social support.

November's inflation trends offer a microcosm of the broader economic challenges facing the UK. The rise in CPI to 2.6%, driven by higher fuel and clothing prices, reflects both persistent supply-side pressures and the complexities of navigating post-pandemic recovery. Core and services inflation underscore the structural challenges in achieving price stability, while fiscal and monetary policy responses highlight the difficult trade-offs facing policymakers.

The broader economic context—marked by stagnant growth, declining business confidence, and external vulnerabilities—adds to the urgency of addressing inflation sustainably. As the Bank of England and the government grapple with these challenges, their decisions will have far-reaching implications for economic stability and societal well-being.

Understanding the interplay between inflation trends and economic challenges is critical for crafting effective policies that balance growth, stability, and equity.

Chapter 1:

Key Drivers of Inflation Increase

Inflation is a critical economic indicator that affects all facets of a nation's economy. It influences purchasing power, business profitability, and monetary policy decisions. The rise in the United Kingdom's inflation rate to 2.6% in November, from 2.3% in October, underscores the complexity of addressing inflationary pressures in a dynamic economic environment. Among the notable drivers of this increase are the prices of motor fuels and clothing, alongside the broader influences of core inflation and services inflation. This chapter delves into these key drivers, examining their impacts and underlying causes to provide a comprehensive understanding of their roles in the inflationary uptick.

Impact of Motor Fuels and Clothing Prices

Motor Fuels: A Volatile Component

Motor fuel prices are among the most volatile elements contributing to inflation. In November, higher fuel costs played a significant role in driving the consumer price index (CPI) upward. The volatility in motor fuel prices can often be attributed to fluctuations in global crude oil prices, geopolitical tensions, and supply chain disruptions.

For instance, global crude oil prices surged in late 2023 due to reduced output from major oil-producing nations, including OPEC members. This supply constraint, coupled with heightened demand as economies continued to recover from pandemic-induced slowdowns, created a pricing pressure felt acutely by consumers at the pump. The UK, being heavily reliant on imported oil, experienced a direct transmission of these global price hikes to domestic fuel costs.

Additionally, the UK government's green energy policies and fuel duties have added layers of complexity. While these policies aim to reduce carbon emissions, they often translate into higher costs for fossil fuels, further exacerbating inflationary pressures. For businesses reliant on logistics and transportation, increased fuel prices raise operational costs, which are frequently passed on to consumers through higher prices for goods and services. This ripple effect contributes to a broader inflationary environment.

Clothing Prices: Seasonal and Supply Chain Influences

Clothing prices also emerged as a significant contributor to November's inflation increase. The rise can be partially attributed to seasonal trends, as retailers often adjust prices during the lead-up to the holiday shopping season. However, underlying supply chain disruptions and increased production costs have also played a pivotal role.

Global supply chain challenges, including port congestion, shipping delays, and higher freight costs, have strained the apparel industry. Many UK retailers rely on international suppliers, particularly from Asia, where production costs have risen due to labor shortages and higher raw material prices. These factors have forced retailers to raise prices to maintain profitability.

Moreover, the depreciation of the pound sterling against major currencies has compounded these challenges. A weaker currency increases the cost of imports, including textiles and finished clothing items, directly influencing retail prices. While demand for clothing remains robust, especially during festive periods, consumers are facing higher price tags, which contributes to overall inflation.

Role of Core Inflation and Services Inflation

Core Inflation: A Measure of Underlying Pressures.

Core inflation, which excludes volatile components such as energy, food, alcohol, and tobacco, provides a clearer picture of persistent price pressures within an economy. In

November, core inflation in the UK rose to 3.5%, up from 3.3% in October, signaling underlying issues beyond short-term price shocks.

One significant factor driving core inflation is wage growth. Over the past year, the UK has seen an acceleration in wage increases across various sectors, partly due to labor shortages and rising living costs. While higher wages support consumer spending, they also increase production costs for businesses, leading to higher prices for goods and services. This wage-price spiral can sustain inflationary pressures, making them harder to control.

Additionally, housing costs, including rent and owner-occupied housing expenses, have contributed to core inflation. The UK's housing market remains tight, with demand outstripping supply in many regions. Rising rents and associated costs have added to households' financial burdens, further pushing up core inflation metrics.

Services Inflation: A Persistent Challenge

Services inflation, a key metric monitored by the Bank of England (BoE), remained stubbornly high at 5% in November, matching October's figure. Services inflation reflects price changes in non-goods sectors such as healthcare, education, hospitality, and financial services. Its persistence is a significant concern for policymakers as it indicates entrenched domestic price pressures.

The services sector, which constitutes a substantial portion of the UK economy, has faced rising input costs, particularly wages. Labor-intensive industries such as hospitality and healthcare have experienced acute staff shortages, compelling employers to offer higher salaries and benefits to attract workers. These increased costs are often transferred to consumers, resulting in higher service prices.

Moreover, regulatory changes, such as increases in employer national insurance contributions, have amplified cost pressures for businesses in the services sector. These additional expenses are particularly impactful for industries with high labor-to-revenue ratios, such as education and healthcare. Consequently, the BoE's efforts to bring services inflation closer to its 2% target face significant headwinds.

Another contributing factor is the growing demand for certain services in the post-pandemic economy. For instance, the surge in travel and leisure activities has allowed businesses in these sectors to raise prices without significantly deterring demand. This pricing power, combined with elevated input costs, has sustained high services inflation.

Interplay Between Key Drivers

The interaction between motor fuels, clothing prices, core inflation, and services inflation creates a complex inflationary landscape. For example, higher fuel prices not only impact transportation costs but also influence the cost of delivering goods and services across industries. Similarly, rising wages contribute to both core and services inflation by increasing production and operational expenses.

The interconnected nature of these drivers underscores the challenges faced by the Bank of England in managing inflation. While addressing one component, such as fuel prices, may offer temporary relief, persistent pressures in wages or services costs can offset these gains, making a comprehensive policy approach essential.

Implications for Policymakers and Consumers

For policymakers, the November inflation figures highlight the need for a balanced approach. While the Bank of England has prioritized controlling inflation through interest rate adjustments, its ability to do so is constrained by the stagnating economy. Raising interest rates further could dampen economic activity, exacerbating challenges for households and businesses already grappling with higher costs.

For consumers, the rising cost of living continues to strain household budgets. The increase in essential expenses, such as fuel, clothing, and services, leaves less disposable income for other needs, potentially dampening consumer confidence and spending. This dynamic poses risks to broader economic growth.

The rise in UK inflation to 2.6% in November is a multifaceted issue driven by both global and domestic factors. Motor fuels and clothing prices have played prominent roles, influenced by supply chain disruptions, currency fluctuations, and seasonal demand. Meanwhile, core inflation and services inflation reflect deeper, more persistent challenges tied to wage growth, housing costs, and sector-specific dynamics.

Understanding these key drivers is crucial for designing effective policy responses and managing the economic impacts of inflation. As the Bank of England navigates these complexities, it must balance its mandate to control inflation with the broader goal of sustaining economic stability. Similarly, businesses and consumers will need to adapt to an environment of heightened cost pressures, emphasizing the importance of resilience and strategic planning in the face of inflationary challenges.

Chapter 2:

Bank of England's Monetary Policy Response

Monetary Policy Committee Meeting Outlook

The Bank of England (BoE) faces an increasingly complex challenge in managing its monetary policy amid persistent inflation and a stagnating economy. November's inflation data, which saw the Consumer Price Index (CPI) rise to 2.6 percent from October's 2.3 percent, underscores the precarious balancing act that the BoE's Monetary Policy Committee (MPC) must perform. With inflation hovering above the BoE's 2 percent target, the MPC's meeting in December is widely anticipated to hold interest rates steady at 4.75 percent. However, this decision will not be made in isolation but against the backdrop of broader economic factors, including weak growth, tepid business confidence, and labor market uncertainties.

The MPC's task is further complicated by the mixed signals emanating from the economy. While inflation has decreased significantly from its peak of 11.1 percent in October 2022, the recent uptick in CPI and a parallel rise in wage growth suggest that inflationary pressures remain entrenched. This has quashed hopes for an immediate interest rate cut, forcing the MPC to tread cautiously.

The BoE's Governor, Andrew Bailey, has reiterated that the central bank will pursue a gradual approach to monetary easing. However, the persistence of core inflation, particularly in the services sector, has fueled concerns within the MPC about the sustainability of the current inflation trajectory. The November services inflation figure of 5 percent, while stable compared to October, still exceeded the BoE's forecast of 4.9 percent, adding to the committee's apprehensions.

One critical factor shaping the MPC's outlook is the global economic environment. Slowing growth in major economies, including the Eurozone and the United States, presents risks to the UK's export-driven sectors. At the same time, geopolitical uncertainties and volatile energy markets continue to impact consumer prices. These external pressures amplify the MPC's domestic challenge of achieving price stability while supporting economic growth.

Another focal point for the MPC is fiscal policy. The tax-raising budget announced in October by Chancellor Rachel Reeves has introduced new variables into the inflation equation. The rise in employer national insurance contributions, coupled with other tax measures, is expected to increase business costs, particularly in the labor-intensive services sector. This fiscal backdrop influences the MPC's decisions, as it must consider the potential inflationary impact of higher business costs alongside the deflationary effects of weaker consumer demand.

As the MPC convenes, one of its primary tasks will be to assess the medium-term inflation outlook. Policymakers must weigh the risks of tightening monetary policy too quickly against the dangers of allowing inflation expectations to become unanchored. The BoE's credibility in maintaining its inflation target hinges on its ability to communicate a clear and consistent strategy to markets and the public. The December meeting, therefore, serves as a critical juncture for the MPC to reinforce its commitment to price stability while signaling its readiness to adapt to evolving economic conditions.

Interest Rate Trends and Market Expectations

Interest rate trends have emerged as a central theme in the UK's economic discourse, reflecting the complex interplay between inflation dynamics, economic growth, and market sentiment. Over the past year, the BoE has adjusted its monetary policy stance multiple times to address shifting economic conditions. From a peak interest rate of 5.25 percent earlier in the year, the BoE has implemented two rate cuts, bringing the rate to its current level of 4.75 percent. These moves were aimed at providing some relief to borrowers and supporting economic activity in the face of slowing GDP growth.

However, the recent inflation data has significantly altered market expectations. Investors now anticipate that the BoE will maintain its current rate at the December MPC meeting, with swaps markets reflecting little probability of an interest rate cut in the near term. This shift in sentiment underscores the challenge of reconciling the need for monetary easing with the imperative of containing inflation.

Historically, interest rate decisions by the BoE have been closely linked to its inflation target of 2 percent. When inflation rises above this threshold, the central bank typically increases rates to curb demand and bring price growth under control. Conversely, when inflation falls below target, rate cuts are employed to stimulate economic activity. In the current environment, however, this traditional framework is being tested by the coexistence of high inflation and weak growth – a phenomenon often described as stagflation.

One of the key drivers of market expectations is the labor market. Recent data showing a rise in wage growth has heightened concerns about a potential wage-price spiral, where higher wages feed into rising prices, perpetuating inflationary pressures. The BoE's policymakers have expressed caution in interpreting these figures, noting that wage growth may not fully reflect underlying economic conditions.

Nevertheless, the persistence of high wage inflation adds another layer of complexity to the MPC's deliberations.

Another factor influencing interest rate trends is the exchange rate. Following the release of the November inflation figures, sterling edged down 0.1 percent to $1.269, reflecting subdued market confidence. A weaker currency can exacerbate inflation by increasing the cost of imports, particularly energy and raw materials. This dynamic places additional pressure on the BoE to maintain a tight monetary stance, even as economic growth remains sluggish.

Market participants are also closely watching global interest rate trends, particularly in the United States and the Eurozone. Central banks in these regions have adopted varying approaches to monetary policy in response to their own inflation challenges. For instance, the U.S. Federal Reserve has signaled a pause in rate hikes, while the European Central Bank has indicated a more cautious approach to monetary easing. These divergent strategies create spillover effects for the UK, influencing capital flows and exchange rate dynamics.

Looking ahead, market expectations suggest a cautious trajectory for UK interest rates. While the BoE is unlikely to cut rates in the immediate term, investors anticipate two reductions in 2024 as inflationary pressures ease and growth concerns take center stage. This forecast reflects a broader consensus that the BoE's monetary policy will remain data-dependent, with decisions guided by the evolving balance of risks to inflation and growth.

The BoE's communication strategy will play a crucial role in shaping market expectations. Clear and transparent messaging about the central bank's policy intentions can help reduce uncertainty and anchor inflation expectations. Governor Bailey and other MPC members have emphasized the importance of gradualism and flexibility, signaling that the BoE stands ready to adjust its stance as needed to achieve its dual mandate of price stability and economic growth.

In conclusion, the BoE's monetary policy response reflects a delicate balancing act between addressing persistent inflation and supporting a fragile economy. The December MPC meeting will be pivotal in setting the tone for the coming year, with interest rate trends and market expectations serving as key indicators of the central bank's strategy. As the UK navigates a period of economic uncertainty, the BoE's actions will have far-reaching implications for businesses, households, and the broader economy.

Chapter 3:

Economic Context and Challenges

Shrinking GDP and Business Confidence

The economic context in which the United Kingdom finds itself has been marked by a combination of shrinking GDP and wavering business confidence. These factors collectively highlight the fragility of the nation's economic health and the challenges policymakers face in steering the economy toward stability and growth.

Shrinking GDP: A Cause for Concern

Gross Domestic Product (GDP) serves as a primary indicator of economic health, reflecting the total value of goods and services produced within a country over a specific period. Recent figures show that the UK's GDP has contracted for two consecutive months, signaling a troubling trend. This contraction reflects reduced economic activity and is a stark reminder of the broader macroeconomic challenges facing the nation.

One of the primary drivers of the GDP decline has been sluggish performance in key sectors such as manufacturing and retail. The manufacturing sector has been hampered by supply chain disruptions, higher production costs, and weaker demand both domestically and internationally. Retail, a critical pillar of the UK economy, has also suffered due to reduced consumer spending power amid rising living costs. As inflation erodes disposable income, households have become more cautious in their spending habits, prioritizing essentials over discretionary purchases.

The economic stagnation is further exacerbated by weak global economic conditions. The UK, as a globally integrated economy, is not insulated from external shocks. Slower growth in major trading partners such as the European Union, the United States, and China has dampened export performance, contributing to the overall contraction in GDP.

Business Confidence Under Strain

Business confidence, a crucial driver of investment and economic activity, has also taken a significant hit. Surveys of business leaders reveal a growing sense of pessimism, with many citing economic uncertainty, higher taxes, and inflationary pressures as key concerns. This lack of confidence is evident in curtailed hiring plans, reduced capital expenditures, and a general hesitancy to expand operations.

The chilling effect on business confidence can be attributed to several interrelated factors. Firstly, persistent inflation has raised the cost of inputs, squeezing profit margins for businesses across various industries. Secondly, the tax-raising measures introduced in the October Budget have added to the financial burden on companies, particularly small and medium-sized enterprises (SMEs). Finally, political and regulatory uncertainty has created an environment in which businesses are reluctant to take risks.

One notable consequence of waning business confidence is a slowdown in job creation. Companies, wary of the economic outlook, have adopted a more cautious approach to hiring. This has implications for the labor market, potentially leading to higher unemployment and reduced wage growth, further impacting consumer confidence and spending.

Impact on the Services Sector

The services sector, which accounts for a significant portion of the UK's GDP, has been particularly vulnerable to these challenges. As a labor-intensive industry, services businesses are heavily affected by rising costs, including wages, energy prices, and taxes. The contraction in services activity has a ripple effect across the economy, given the sector's interconnectedness with other industries.

Impact of Rachel Reeves' Budget on Hiring and Inflation

The October Budget, presented by Chancellor of the Exchequer Rachel Reeves, introduced several measures aimed at addressing fiscal challenges and raising revenue. While these policies were intended to stabilize public finances, they have had notable repercussions on hiring and inflation, raising questions about their long-term implications for the economy.

Key Provisions of the Budget

Reeves' Budget included a series of tax-raising measures designed to generate additional government revenue. Among the most significant were:

1. **Increase in National Insurance Contributions:** Employers faced higher national insurance contributions, a move aimed at bolstering the social security system but one that added to business costs.
2. **Corporate Tax Adjustments:** Changes in corporate tax rates and allowances were implemented, impacting the profitability of businesses.
3. **Targeted Sectoral Taxes:** Certain industries, such as financial services and energy, were subjected to additional levies, reflecting the government's focus on tapping into high-profit sectors.
4. **Reduced Investment Incentives:** Some tax reliefs and incentives for business investment were scaled back, potentially discouraging capital expenditure.

Effects on Hiring

The higher national insurance contributions announced in the Budget have had a pronounced effect on hiring intentions. Employers, particularly those in labor-intensive sectors such as retail, hospitality, and healthcare, have expressed concerns about the added financial burden. For many businesses, these additional costs translate to a reduced capacity to hire new staff or retain existing employees.

The services sector has been disproportionately affected due to its reliance on human capital. Employers in this sector face difficult choices: either absorb the higher costs, which erodes profitability, or pass them on to consumers, which could further dampen demand. In many cases, businesses have opted to scale back hiring plans, contributing to the broader economic slowdown.

Small and medium-sized enterprises (SMEs), which are vital to job creation, have been particularly vulnerable to the higher costs imposed by the Budget. Unlike larger corporations, SMEs often lack the financial resilience to weather such changes, leading to staff reductions or hiring freezes. This has implications not only for unemployment rates but also for overall economic dynamism, as SMEs are typically engines of innovation and growth.

Inflationary Pressures

The Budget's impact on inflation has been a contentious issue among economists and policymakers. While the measures were designed to address fiscal imbalances, they have inadvertently contributed to inflationary pressures in several ways:

1. **Increased Business Costs:** Higher taxes on employers, including national insurance contributions, have raised the cost structure for many businesses. These costs are often passed on to consumers in the form of higher prices, fueling inflation.
2. **Wage Pressures:** In response to the higher cost of living, employees have demanded higher wages. This has created a wage-price spiral, where rising wages lead to increased costs for businesses, which in turn are passed on to consumers.
3. **Sectoral Impacts:** The targeted taxes on industries such as energy and financial services have had sector-specific inflationary effects. For example, higher energy costs

directly impact households and businesses, contributing to overall inflation.

4. **Reduced Consumer Spending Power:** By raising taxes on businesses and households, the Budget has reduced disposable income, leading to a shift in spending patterns. While this may dampen demand for certain goods and services, it also creates inflationary pressures in essential sectors where demand remains inelastic.

Policy Debate and Criticism

The measures introduced in the Budget have sparked significant debate among economists, policymakers, and business leaders. Critics argue that the timing of the tax increases was poorly chosen, given the fragile state of the economy. They contend that the additional financial burden on businesses and households risks exacerbating the economic slowdown and undermining recovery efforts.

Opposition parties have been vocal in their criticism, with Conservative shadow chancellor Mel Stride accusing Reeves of making "irresponsible and inflationary decisions." Stride and others have argued that the Budget's measures could lead to a prolonged period of higher inflation, complicating the Bank of England's efforts to achieve its 2 percent inflation target.

Long-Term Implications

The long-term implications of Reeves' Budget on hiring and inflation remain uncertain. While the measures were intended to address fiscal sustainability, their impact on economic growth and stability could undermine these goals. Policymakers face the difficult task of balancing fiscal discipline with the need to support economic activity.

One potential silver lining is that the higher tax revenues generated by the Budget could provide the government with additional resources to invest in infrastructure, education, and other areas that support long-term growth. However, such benefits will take time to materialize and may not offset the short-term challenges posed by the measures.

The UK's economic context is characterized by shrinking GDP, weakened business confidence, and the far-reaching effects of fiscal policies such as Rachel Reeves' Budget. The interplay of these factors highlights the complexity of managing an economy in a period of uncertainty and persistent inflationary pressures.

Addressing these challenges will require a coordinated approach that balances the need for fiscal discipline with measures to support growth and stability. Policymakers must carefully consider the implications of their decisions on businesses, households, and the broader economy to navigate this challenging period effectively.

Chapter 4:

Stakeholder Perspectives

The interplay between inflation, monetary policy, and economic stability is a subject of intense scrutiny and debate among various stakeholders. In the United Kingdom, the sharp rise in inflation in

November to 2.6%, combined with broader economic challenges, has sparked diverse opinions from economic experts and government officials. Their perspectives shed light on the underlying causes of inflation, the appropriateness of current policy responses, and the broader implications for the economy.

Commentary from Economic Experts

Economic experts have been vocal about the implications of the latest inflation data and the broader trends it signals. Their insights provide a nuanced understanding of the inflationary pressures and the potential trajectory of the UK economy.

Suren Thiru: Inflation Risks and Policy Implications

Suren Thiru, economics director at the Institute of Chartered Accountants in England and Wales (ICAEW), highlighted the persistence of inflationary risks despite recent policy adjustments by the Bank of England (BoE). According to Thiru, the uptick in the consumer price index (CPI) to 2.6% in November effectively nullifies any immediate hopes for an interest rate cut during the BoE's December meeting. He pointed to mounting risks, including rising wage growth, as critical factors reinforcing inflationary pressures.

Thiru's analysis underscores the complexity of the BoE's challenge. While interest rate reductions could alleviate borrowing costs and stimulate economic activity, they might also exacerbate inflationary pressures if implemented prematurely. His comments also raise concerns about the likelihood of additional policy loosening in early 2024, suggesting that the path to stable inflation remains fraught with uncertainty.

Paul Dales: Forecasting Higher Inflation

Paul Dales of Capital Economics offered a similarly cautionary perspective. He argued that the recent inflation figures, combined with wage growth dynamics, could keep inflation nearly a point above the BoE's 2% target into early 2024. Dales' assessment highlights a key challenge for policymakers: managing inflation while navigating a stagnant economy.

Dales also emphasized the long-term implications of rising inflation. He noted that core inflation—excluding volatile components like energy and food—has remained stubbornly high.

This persistence suggests that inflationary pressures are not solely driven by temporary external shocks but are embedded within the domestic economy. For instance, services inflation, a critical indicator of underlying price pressures, has stayed elevated due to rising labor costs and other structural factors.

Andrew Wishart: The Services Sector's Role

Andrew Wishart, an economist at Berenberg Bank, focused on the services sector as a significant contributor to inflation. According to Wishart, the rise in employer national insurance contributions announced by Rachel Reeves has intensified cost pressures for service-based businesses. Given that labor constitutes a substantial portion of costs in the services sector, the increased financial burden on employers could perpetuate high inflation in services prices.

Wishart's analysis raises important questions about the sustainability of current inflation trends. Historically, a 3% increase in services prices has aligned with the BoE's inflation target. However, the current rate—well above 5%—indicates a prolonged deviation from target levels. Wishart's comments suggest that achieving the 2% inflation target will require both monetary and fiscal policy interventions to address structural cost pressures in the services sector.

Clare Lombardelli: Persistent Inflationary Pressures

Clare Lombardelli, the deputy governor of the BoE, has also expressed concerns about the persistence of inflationary pressures, particularly in the services sector. In an interview with the Financial Times, Lombardelli highlighted that services inflation has remained "well above" rates consistent with the BoE's 2% target. She attributed this trend to sustained wage growth and other domestic factors, which have offset the disinflationary impact of declining energy prices.

Lombardelli's perspective underscores the importance of a cautious approach to monetary policy. While gradual easing may be necessary to support economic growth, the persistence of services inflation demands vigilance. Her comments suggest that the BoE's future policy decisions will need to strike a delicate balance between fostering economic recovery and maintaining price stability.

Statements from Government Officials

Government officials have weighed in on the latest inflation data, offering diverse perspectives on its causes and implications. Their statements reflect a broader debate about the role of fiscal policy, structural reforms, and other government interventions in addressing inflationary challenges.

Rachel Reeves: Fighting for Working People

Rachel Reeves, the Shadow Chancellor of the Exchequer, has framed the inflation debate within the context of her broader economic agenda. In a statement responding to the November inflation figures, Reeves acknowledged the ongoing struggles faced by families due to the rising cost of living. She emphasized her commitment to "putting more money in the pockets of working people" and outlined the need for policies that promote economic equity.

Reeves' approach has focused on addressing structural issues that contribute to inflationary pressures. Her proposed tax reforms, including the increase in national insurance contributions for employers, aim to fund critical public services while ensuring a fairer distribution of wealth. However, critics have argued that these measures may inadvertently exacerbate inflation by raising business costs.

Mel Stride: Criticism of Inflationary Decisions

Mel Stride, the Conservative Shadow Chancellor, has been a vocal critic of Reeves' policies, accusing her of making "a series of irresponsible and inflationary decisions." Stride's critique centers on the potential inflationary impact of higher taxes and increased employer contributions, which he argues could stifle economic growth and prolong inflation.

Stride's comments highlight a key tension in the inflation debate: the trade-off between fiscal responsibility and economic stimulus. While Reeves' policies aim to address structural inequalities, Stride contends that they risk undermining business confidence and investment. This divergence reflects broader ideological differences about the role of government in managing inflation and fostering economic stability.

Andrew Bailey: Gradual Policy Adjustments

Andrew Bailey, the Governor of the Bank of England, has reiterated the importance of a measured approach to monetary policy. In recent statements, Bailey has emphasized that the BoE will continue to ease policy gradually, balancing the need to support economic growth with the imperative to contain inflation.

Bailey's stance reflects a recognition of the complex interplay between monetary and fiscal policies. While the BoE's interest rate decisions are critical for managing inflation expectations, Bailey has also called for complementary measures from the government to address structural cost pressures. His comments suggest that a coordinated approach—involving both monetary and fiscal policies—is essential for achieving long-term price stability.

Broader Government Responses

Other government officials have also weighed in on the inflation debate, emphasizing the need for targeted interventions to support vulnerable populations. For instance, proposals for increased energy subsidies and expanded social welfare programs have been floated as potential measures to alleviate the impact of rising prices on low-income households.

At the same time, there is growing recognition of the need to address supply-side constraints that contribute to inflation. Initiatives to enhance workforce productivity, reduce regulatory burdens, and promote investment in critical sectors such as housing and energy have been identified as key priorities. These measures aim to address the root causes of inflation while fostering long-term economic resilience.

The perspectives of economic experts and government officials provide a comprehensive view of the challenges and opportunities associated with the current inflationary environment in the UK. While experts emphasize the persistence of inflationary pressures and the need for cautious policy adjustments, government officials have articulated diverse strategies for addressing these challenges.

The ongoing debate underscores the complexity of managing inflation in a stagnating economy. Achieving price stability will require a coordinated effort involving both monetary and fiscal policies, as well as targeted interventions to address structural issues. By balancing these priorities, stakeholders can work toward fostering economic stability and improving the well-being of all citizens.

Chapter 5:

Long-Term Inflationary Concerns

Persistence of Services Inflation

The persistence of services inflation remains a critical concern for policymakers, businesses, and consumers alike. Services inflation, distinct from goods inflation, is primarily driven by wage growth, labor costs, and other domestically rooted factors. This makes it particularly sticky and difficult to control, especially when compared to the often volatile prices of goods influenced by global supply chain dynamics. In November, services inflation in the UK stood at 5%, underscoring the Bank of England's ongoing challenge of bringing this measure closer to its 2% target.

One of the primary reasons services inflation tends to persist is its reliance on human capital. Unlike goods, services are inherently labor-intensive. Whether it's healthcare, education, hospitality, or financial services, the cost of wages constitutes a significant portion of total expenses. When wages rise, service providers often pass these costs onto consumers, leading to higher prices. In the current economic climate, a combination of tight labor markets and rising wage demands has exacerbated these pressures. Wage growth, particularly in industries like healthcare and technology, has remained robust, signaling that services inflation will not abate easily.

Another factor driving the persistence of services inflation is the influence of expectations. Businesses and consumers anticipate future inflation and act accordingly, embedding these expectations into pricing and wage-setting behavior. For instance, if companies expect higher operating costs due to increased wages or taxes, they may preemptively raise prices. Similarly, workers may demand higher wages to keep pace with anticipated cost-of-living increases. This self-reinforcing cycle makes it challenging for central banks like the Bank of England to break the inflationary spiral.

The impact of persistent services inflation extends beyond households and businesses; it complicates monetary policy decisions. The Bank of England's primary tool for controlling inflation is interest rates. However, when services inflation is driven by structural factors—such as demographic changes, skill shortages, or entrenched wage growth—higher interest rates may have limited effectiveness. For example, raising borrowing costs might dampen consumer spending on discretionary goods but have little immediate impact on sectors like healthcare or education, where demand remains inelastic.

Historically, the Bank of England has viewed services inflation as a critical gauge of underlying price pressures. This is because services inflation is less influenced by external shocks, such as fluctuating energy prices or currency movements, and more reflective of domestic economic conditions. In November, the 5% services inflation rate was slightly above the central bank's forecast of 4.9%, reinforcing concerns about the durability of these pressures. The persistence of services inflation, coupled with broader inflationary trends, suggests that achieving the 2% target will require sustained and coordinated policy efforts.

National Insurance Contributions and Services Sector Costs

Another significant contributor to long-term inflationary concerns in the UK is the rise in National Insurance Contributions (NICs), particularly for employers. Introduced as part of Rachel Reeves' budget measures, the increase in employer NICs has added to the financial burden of businesses, especially in the services sector, where labor costs are a dominant expense.

National Insurance is a mandatory tax on earnings, and the burden falls both on employees and employers. The recent increase in employer contributions has sparked widespread debate about its inflationary implications. For businesses in labor-intensive industries such as retail, hospitality, and healthcare, higher NICs mean increased operating costs. Given the thin profit margins in many of these sectors, businesses are often left with two options: absorb the costs, which risks eroding profitability, or pass them onto consumers through higher prices. Both scenarios have inflationary consequences.

Services businesses are particularly vulnerable to these pressures due to the composition of their cost structures. Unlike manufacturing or technology companies that can invest in automation or offshore operations to reduce labor dependence, services firms rely heavily on human resources. For example, a restaurant's ability to serve customers, a hospital's capacity to treat patients, or a school's capability to educate students hinges almost entirely on its workforce. When employer NICs rise, the cost implications are immediate and pronounced, further fueling services inflation.

The timing of the NIC increase has compounded its impact. The UK economy is already grappling with sluggish growth, reduced business investment, and post-pandemic labor market disruptions. Adding to these challenges, the hike in employer NICs has created additional strain on services businesses. Many small and medium-sized enterprises (SMEs), which form the backbone of the UK's services sector, are particularly affected. Unlike larger corporations with diversified revenue streams and stronger financial reserves, SMEs often operate on tight budgets, making it harder for them to absorb rising costs.

From a macroeconomic perspective, the NIC increase also risks undermining employment growth in the services sector. Faced with higher labor costs, some businesses may opt to freeze hiring, reduce working hours, or even lay off employees. This could have a ripple effect on consumer spending and overall economic activity, further complicating the inflationary landscape. Additionally, reduced hiring activity could exacerbate existing labor shortages in key sectors, driving wages higher and perpetuating the cycle of services inflation.

The rise in employer NICs also has implications for monetary policy. Central banks like the Bank of England typically focus on demand-side measures to control inflation, such as adjusting interest rates or influencing credit availability. However, supply-side factors, such as tax increases, require a different set of policy responses. For instance, targeted fiscal interventions—such as tax breaks or subsidies for affected industries—could help mitigate the inflationary impact of higher NICs. Alternatively, the government could explore ways to offset the cost burden on businesses, such as reducing regulatory red tape or providing incentives for workforce development.

Critics of the NIC increase argue that it is a counterproductive measure at a time when the economy needs support, not additional burdens. Mel Stride, the Conservative shadow chancellor, has accused Rachel Reeves of making "irresponsible and inflationary decisions" that risk derailing economic recovery. From this perspective, the NIC hike not only exacerbates inflationary pressures but also undermines business confidence, making it harder for the UK to achieve sustainable growth.

Despite these challenges, proponents of the NIC increase contend that it is a necessary step to fund critical public services and address long-term fiscal imbalances. National Insurance contributions play a vital role in financing the NHS, state pensions, and other welfare programs. In this context, the additional revenue generated by higher employer NICs could help strengthen the social safety net and support vulnerable populations. However, balancing these objectives with the need to control inflation and support economic growth remains a delicate task.

Broader Implications for Inflation and Economic Policy

The interplay between persistent services inflation and rising employer NICs underscores the complexity of managing long-term inflationary concerns in the UK. Policymakers must navigate a delicate balance between addressing short-term inflationary pressures and implementing structural reforms to ensure long-term economic stability. This requires a coordinated approach that integrates monetary, fiscal, and regulatory policies.

One potential avenue for addressing services inflation is enhancing labor market efficiency. By investing in workforce training and education, the government can help address skill shortages and reduce upward pressure on wages. Additionally, promoting greater labor market flexibility—such as through remote work options or flexible scheduling—could help mitigate the cost pressures faced by services businesses.

Another key priority is fostering innovation and productivity in the services sector. Historically, productivity growth in services has lagged behind that of goods-producing industries. By encouraging the adoption of digital technologies, automation, and process improvements, businesses can reduce their reliance on labor-intensive practices and better manage costs. For example, the use of artificial intelligence in customer service or telemedicine in healthcare has the potential to enhance efficiency and reduce inflationary pressures.

On the fiscal side, targeted measures to support services businesses could play a crucial role in mitigating the impact of rising NICs. For instance, tax incentives for businesses that invest in workforce development or digital transformation could help offset the additional costs associated with higher employer contributions. Similarly, policies aimed at reducing energy costs or other non-labor expenses could provide much-needed relief to services firms.

Finally, effective communication and coordination between policymakers and stakeholders are essential for addressing long-term inflationary concerns. The Bank of England, government agencies, and industry representatives must work together to develop comprehensive strategies that address the root causes of inflation while supporting economic growth. This includes fostering an open dialogue on the implications of policy decisions and ensuring that businesses and consumers have the information they need to plan effectively.

Conclusion

Long-term inflationary concerns in the UK, driven by persistent services inflation and rising employer National Insurance Contributions, pose significant challenges for policymakers and businesses. The structural nature of these issues—rooted in labor market dynamics, cost structures, and fiscal policies—requires a multifaceted approach to ensure sustainable economic stability.

Addressing these challenges will require a combination of targeted interventions, such as promoting labor market efficiency, fostering innovation, and providing fiscal support to affected industries. At the same time, policymakers must remain vigilant in monitoring inflation trends and adapting their strategies as needed. By taking a proactive and coordinated approach, the UK can navigate the complexities of long-term inflationary pressures and lay the groundwork for a more resilient and inclusive economy.

Chapter 6:

Forecasts and Projections

Inflation Trajectory for Early 2024

The inflation outlook for the United Kingdom as it moves into early 2024 presents a complex scenario marked by a delicate balancing act between ongoing price pressures and economic stagnation. While inflation has significantly cooled from its peak of 11.1% in October 2022, the recent uptick in the Consumer Price Index (CPI) to 2.6% in November 2023 highlights the persistence of underlying inflationary forces. This resurgence poses fresh challenges for policymakers, businesses, and consumers alike.

Key Indicators of Inflation Trends

As of November 2023, the core inflation rate, which excludes volatile items such as energy, food, alcohol, and tobacco, stood at 3.5%, up from 3.3% in October. Similarly, services inflation remained elevated at 5%, reflecting robust price pressures in domestic, labor-intensive sectors. These figures underscore that while headline inflation has eased, the underlying trends remain stubbornly above the Bank of England's (BoE) 2% target.

Economists widely predict that inflation will hover around 3% to 3.5% in the first quarter of 2024, with specific sectors, such as services and housing, contributing disproportionately. Paul Dales of Capital Economics has forecasted that inflation could be nearly a point above the BoE's target early next year, a development that complicates the central bank's decision-making process.

Contributing Factors to Inflation Persistence

1. **Wage Growth:** Recent data show a marked increase in wage growth, driven by tight labor market conditions and higher national insurance contributions. Rising wages often lead to increased consumer spending, which in turn fuels demand-driven inflation. This dynamic has raised concerns about a potential wage-price spiral, where higher wages lead to higher prices and vice versa.
2. **Services Sector Dynamics:** The services sector, which constitutes a significant portion of the UK economy,

continues to grapple with elevated inflation rates. Historically, a 3% increase in services prices has been consistent with the BoE's inflation target. However, the current rate of 5% signals entrenched price pressures, influenced by higher staff costs and increased operating expenses.

3. **Impact of Fiscal Policies:** Measures introduced in Rachel Reeves' tax-raising budget, including the rise in employer national insurance contributions, are expected to exert upward pressure on inflation. These costs are likely to be passed on to consumers, particularly in service-based industries, thereby sustaining elevated price levels.

4. **Global and Domestic Supply Chains:** While supply chain disruptions have eased compared to the pandemic years, certain global factors, such as higher energy prices and geopolitical tensions, continue to exert inflationary pressures. Domestically, Brexit-related trade frictions remain a long-term challenge, particularly in the food and manufacturing sectors.

Sectoral Outlook

1. **Energy Prices:** Although energy prices have moderated from their 2022 highs, volatility in global oil and gas markets remains a risk. Any unexpected supply shocks could quickly translate into higher costs for businesses and households.
2. **Food Inflation:** Food prices, which have been a significant contributor to headline inflation, are expected to stabilize but remain above pre-pandemic levels due to persistent supply chain inefficiencies and higher import costs.
3. **Housing Market:** Rising mortgage costs, driven by previous interest rate hikes, continue to weigh on household budgets. While this dampens consumer spending in some areas, it also contributes to sustained inflationary pressures in rent and housing-related services.

Potential Policy Adjustments by the Bank of England

The Bank of England faces a challenging task as it navigates the complex interplay of slowing economic growth and persistent inflation. With inflation still above target and GDP contracting for two consecutive months, the BoE's Monetary Policy Committee (MPC) must weigh the risks of tightening monetary policy further against the potential economic fallout.

Interest Rate Strategy

1. **Current Stance:** The BoE has maintained interest rates at 4.75% following two rate cuts earlier in 2023. This decision reflects the central bank's cautious approach, balancing the need to combat inflation against concerns over economic stagnation.
2. **Future Rate Adjustments:** Given the recent uptick in inflation and robust wage growth, the likelihood of an interest rate cut in early 2024 has diminished significantly. Instead, the BoE may opt to hold rates steady, providing room to assess the impact of previous adjustments. Suren Thiru, economics director at the ICAEW, noted that the November CPI figure "extinguishes any lingering hopes of an interest rate cut on Thursday, while concerns over mounting inflation risks… mean that a February loosening is not a done deal."

3. **Gradual Easing vs. Prolonged Tightening:** Governor Andrew Bailey has emphasized the importance of a gradual approach to monetary easing. However, the persistence of core and services inflation may necessitate a prolonged period of higher interest rates to anchor inflation expectations. Any premature loosening could risk undermining the central bank's credibility.

Targeting Services Inflation

Services inflation, which is closely monitored by the BoE, has proven particularly resistant to policy measures. Clare Lombardelli, the deputy governor, expressed concern over services price inflation remaining "well above" levels consistent with the 2% target. To address this, the MPC may explore targeted measures, including:

- **Enhanced Communication:** Clear communication about the BoE's inflation targets and monetary policy intentions can help shape market expectations and reduce inflationary pressures.
- **Support for Productivity Growth:** Collaborating with the government to promote productivity-enhancing

investments, particularly in the services sector, could help mitigate cost-push inflation over the medium term.

Quantitative Easing and Financial Stability

1. **Asset Purchase Programs:** While the BoE has reduced its holdings of government bonds as part of its quantitative tightening strategy, the central bank may consider pausing or adjusting this approach if financial stability risks emerge. Any such moves would need to be carefully calibrated to avoid exacerbating inflationary pressures.
2. **Market Liquidity:** Ensuring adequate liquidity in financial markets will remain a priority, particularly if higher interest rates lead to stress in specific sectors, such as housing or small and medium-sized enterprises (SMEs).

Collaboration with Fiscal Policy

The BoE's efforts to control inflation are complemented by fiscal policies implemented by the government. However, recent measures, such as increased national insurance contributions, have raised concerns about their inflationary impact. A coordinated approach between monetary and fiscal authorities will be essential to achieving sustainable economic stability. This could include:

- **Targeted Support for Vulnerable Sectors:** Providing temporary relief to sectors disproportionately affected by inflation, such as services and housing, could help mitigate price pressures without undermining monetary policy objectives.
- **Structural Reforms:** Long-term reforms aimed at improving labor market flexibility, enhancing supply chain resilience, and fostering innovation could address the root causes of inflation and support economic growth.

Risks and Uncertainties

The path of inflation and monetary policy in early 2024 is subject to several uncertainties:

1. **Geopolitical Risks:** Escalating geopolitical tensions or disruptions in global energy markets could lead to renewed inflationary pressures.

2. **Consumer Behavior:** Changes in consumer spending patterns, driven by shifts in sentiment or unexpected economic shocks, could alter the inflation trajectory.
3. **Policy Missteps:** Any misalignment between monetary and fiscal policies could exacerbate economic challenges and prolong inflationary pressures.

Conclusion

The inflation trajectory for early 2024 highlights the complexities of the current economic landscape. While headline inflation has moderated, persistent core and services inflation present significant challenges for the Bank of England. The central bank's cautious approach to monetary policy, coupled with targeted measures to address sector-specific pressures, will be critical in navigating these challenges.

Ultimately, the BoE's ability to anchor inflation expectations and support economic stability will depend on its capacity to adapt to evolving circumstances, foster collaboration with fiscal authorities, and maintain public confidence in its policy framework.

Conclusion

Summary of Inflationary Pressures

The resurgence of inflation in November, as evidenced by the rise in the Consumer Price Index (CPI) to 2.6 percent, underscores the persistent economic challenges faced by the UK. While inflation has moderated significantly from its peak of 11.1 percent in October 2022, the recent uptick highlights the complexity of addressing economic imbalances in an environment fraught with structural and external pressures. This chapter examines the dynamics underpinning inflationary trends and explores their broader implications for economic stability.

One of the primary drivers of November's inflation increase was the rise in prices for motor fuels and clothing. These commodities, essential to household consumption, have proven particularly sensitive to supply chain disruptions, fluctuating global energy prices, and seasonal demand. The impact of motor fuels is especially significant given the UK's reliance on both domestic and imported energy. Meanwhile, clothing prices often reflect broader market trends, including labor costs and international trade tariffs, further exacerbating inflationary pressures.

Core inflation—excluding volatile components such as energy, food, alcohol, and tobacco—rose to 3.5 percent in November from 3.3 percent in October. This increase reveals underlying price pressures that extend beyond transient external shocks. Notably, services inflation remained elevated at 5 percent, underscoring sustained wage growth and rising costs in labor-intensive sectors. The persistence of high services inflation reflects structural rigidities in the economy, where tight labor markets and elevated demand for skilled workers push up wages, which in turn translates into higher prices for services.

The stagnation in GDP over recent months and the subdued business confidence following the government's tax-raising Budget further complicate the inflation narrative. While inflationary pressures are often symptomatic of overheating economies, the UK's case is unique in that inflation coexists with weak economic growth. This stagflationary scenario places policymakers in a bind, as traditional monetary and fiscal tools may prove inadequate or counterproductive.

Policy Implications for Economic Stability

The Bank of England (BoE) has been at the forefront of efforts to tackle inflation while maintaining economic stability. However, its dual mandate of price stability and sustainable economic growth has never been more challenging. The BoE's decision to hold interest rates at 4.75 percent in December—after two rate cuts earlier in the year—illustrates the cautious approach adopted by policymakers in the face of competing economic priorities.

Inflationary pressures necessitate a measured policy response. On one hand, the BoE must curb inflation expectations to prevent a wage-price spiral, where rising wages fuel further price increases. On the other hand, overly restrictive monetary policy risks deepening economic stagnation by dampening investment and consumption. Striking this balance requires a nuanced understanding of inflation drivers and a willingness to adapt policy frameworks as conditions evolve.

The persistence of services inflation is particularly concerning for policymakers. As services account for a significant proportion of the UK economy, the sector's inflationary trends have a disproportionate impact on overall price stability. Deputy Governor Clare Lombardelli's concern over services inflation being "well above" the BoE's 2 percent target reflects a broader consensus among central bank officials regarding the need for vigilance. The BoE's November forecast of 4.9 percent services inflation aligns closely with actual figures, reinforcing the credibility of its predictive models but also highlighting the scale of the challenge.

Beyond monetary policy, fiscal measures play a critical role in shaping inflationary outcomes. The recent Budget, which included an increase in national insurance contributions for employers, has raised concerns about its potential to exacerbate inflationary pressures. The additional cost burden on businesses, particularly in the services sector, is likely to translate into higher prices for consumers, perpetuating the inflationary cycle. As Andrew Wishart of Berenberg Bank notes, achieving a sustainable decline in services inflation requires addressing these structural cost pressures, which currently appear misaligned with the BoE's inflation target.

The role of fiscal policy extends beyond direct cost implications. The government's broader economic strategy, including measures to stimulate growth and support employment, has significant implications for inflation dynamics. Critics have argued that the tax-raising measures in the Budget, while aimed at fiscal consolidation, may have dampened business confidence and curtailed hiring intentions. This chilling effect on economic activity risks creating a feedback loop where weak growth further entrenches inflationary pressures by reducing supply-side flexibility.

Long-Term Considerations

The trajectory of inflation in the UK is shaped by a combination of domestic and global factors. On the global front, energy prices remain a key determinant of inflation volatility. The geopolitical landscape, including ongoing tensions in key energy-producing regions, poses a persistent risk to price stability. Domestically, the labor market and wage growth dynamics will continue to play a crucial role. While wage growth supports household incomes, excessive increases risk entrenching inflation expectations and undermining competitiveness.

The BoE's gradual approach to monetary easing reflects a recognition of these complex interdependencies. While the market anticipates further rate cuts in 2024, policymakers are likely to proceed with caution, particularly if inflation remains above target. The February meeting of the Monetary Policy Committee (MPC) will be closely watched for signals regarding the BoE's medium-term strategy.

Addressing the root causes of inflation requires a coordinated approach that integrates monetary, fiscal, and structural policies. For instance, targeted interventions to enhance productivity in the services sector could help alleviate cost pressures and support sustainable price stability. Similarly, investments in energy efficiency and renewable energy infrastructure could reduce vulnerability to external shocks, providing a more stable foundation for long-term inflation management.

The resurgence of inflation in November serves as a stark reminder of the challenges faced by policymakers in navigating the complex interplay of economic forces. While the recent uptick in inflation is concerning, it also presents an opportunity to reassess and refine the policy frameworks that underpin economic stability. The BoE's cautious approach, combined with targeted fiscal and structural reforms, offers a pathway to achieving sustainable price stability while fostering economic resilience.

Ultimately, addressing inflation requires a holistic perspective that balances short-term priorities with long-term objectives. By fostering a stable macroeconomic environment, the UK can lay the groundwork for a more inclusive and resilient economy, ensuring that the benefits of stability are shared widely across society. This conclusion underscores the importance of vigilance, adaptability, and collaboration in the ongoing effort to tackle inflation and promote economic stability.

www.ingramcontent.com/pod-product-compliance
Lightning Source LLC
Chambersburg PA
CBHW051535240526
45471CB00020B/2677